A Thousand Bright Pieces

A Thousand Bright Pieces

Poems by

Linda Hughes

© 2025 Linda Hughes. All rights reserved.
This material may not be reproduced in any form, published,
reprinted, recorded, performed, broadcast,
rewritten, or redistributed without
the explicit permission of Linda Hughes.
All such actions are strictly prohibited by law.

Cover design by Shay Culligan
Cover art by Abby Warman

ISBN: 978-1-63980-990-5

Kelsay Books
502 South 1040 East, A-119
American Fork, Utah 84003
Kelsaybooks.com

Dedication

I dedicate this book to my eagle-eyed workshop group, Dorothy, Sharon, Lin, and Carol for their gracious help and guidance through the process and especially to my dear husband who is always willing to listen to my first drafts.

Acknowledgments

Thanks to the editors of the following journals in which the listed poems first appeared, some with subtle changes:

Abstract Contemporary Expressions: "A Day Trip Home"
The Avalon Literary Review: "Jane's Eyes"
Broadsides, Art Alliance, Ft. Myers, FL: "Angels in Paris"
The Critical Pass Review: "A Thousand Bright Pieces"
Door Is a Jar: "I Watch My Daughter Smoke"
Drunk Monkeys: "Layers"
The Evening Street Review: "The Shape of My Skin"
Halcyon Days: "A Sip of Wine "
Main Street Rag: "So Much Light"
The Mangrove Review: "Meat"
OVS and The Orchard: "Tie Loosely"
Poetry South: "The Lake Where You Once Proposed"

Contents

Preface	11
A Thousand Bright Pieces	13
When She Left	14
The Mother's Departure	16
So Much Light	17
In a Perfect Dream	18
A Day Trip Home	19
Father and Child in Silhouette	21
The Crepe Myrtle Tree	22
Regrets	23
Petal Pink Lips	24
Meat	25
Chicken Dinner	27
In This Garden	28
Tie Loosely	29
When I First Held My Daughter	30
Swimming Lessons	31
I Watch My Daughter Smoke	32
The Shape of My Skin	33
I Think of You and Forget to Breathe	34
Yellowed Crochet	35
We Stop by the Lake Where You Once Proposed	37
Angels in Paris	38
Jane's Eyes	39
Layers	41
Falling	42
The Pain Body	43
Searching	45
Barefoot with Angels	47
The Color of Her Eyes	49
These Bones I Carry	51
My Mother in Half Shadow	53
Like a Sip of Wine	54

Preface

My mother passed when she was nineteen years old and I was fifteen months. I have written these poems in celebration of my mother who through her death and life facilitated them. Some are not about her but were brought by a way of thinking and seeing through the lens she gave me. They are drawn from overheard conversations, almost forgotten memories, dreams, and places dreams come from. I hope to bring you along with me with your own stories of loss, searching and connection. I wish when you read the poems you find something you have been seeking.

A Thousand Bright Pieces

A memory so clear
it's like a painting lit with sunlight.
You stand in front of ocean waves
holding me.
your face turned toward
the horizon.

The skin of the day
fixed, smoothed tight
across the minutes.
We safe in our bond.

Then a change in the air
like the moment before the music begins
as the maestro raises his arms.

I see a dark spot on the horizon.
I knew then you would leave me.
A child can see things
while still soft from the womb.

The sun close to the water
shows your path.
I see you will not turn
but pass through a loose stitch
between water and sky.

Break into a thousand bright pieces.
Disappear into your own light.

When She Left

He walks the polished hallway,
the sound of his shoes the only thing
that disturbs the quiet.
Then he sees the empty bed,
the stricken look on the preacher's wife's face,
hears her words, "It's too late. She's gone."

An ocean envelops him.
A cold wave spills through like a shock.
He's back in the army.
He's in Burma guiding his troops
through rough waters, hanging on
in rubber boats, jumping from planes
into the thin night, falling, falling,
landing behind enemy lines.
The wave pushes him back up the hall
and sets him on the front steps
of the Saint Frances hospital.
Life again, suddenly strange dark territory.
He trembles and breathes cold January air.

Yesterday he sat in the waiting area,
heard his wife's screams.
No anesthesia was used for these surgeries.
The patient needed to be alert and talking
so vocal cords would not be cut.
He saw the nurses rush out of the surgery,
their aprons covered with blood.

He stayed through the night,
left this morning to clean up and return.
As he left she asked him to pray for her.
He drove to her mother's house with the impossible news.
The grandmother motions toward a child asleep in the next room.
"Oh, what will we do with that baby?"

Over the years when they speak of her death
they say the doctor was a drug addict and an alcoholic.
They say my mother was given too much morphine
after the surgery, or a thyroid storm, a tsunami
of hormones that flooded her body.

The preacher's wife tells me, "Your mother went real easy dear."

The Mother's Departure

I hurt from bruises
      of the surgeon's hands,

cut of his knife.
      The medicine is strong.

I drift, stay too long
      wander so far.

It is calm here above it all.
      I see myself below.

I can't return.
      I reach back.

The door closes.
      I can't leave.

A nurse unfolds a white sheet, covers me.
      They take my body from the room.

I'm too young.
      I call to myself, *Wake up—wake up!*

Transformed, I can't escape.
      My hand on one side of the door,

my heart, the other.

So Much Light

He sits in the dark,
watches her lithe approach.
The door opens
filling the room with light.
She talks to him of time.
Where they could meet inside it.
Unrolls a map of planets and stars
and writing he can't comprehend.
She draws lines from one symbol to another.
Her fingers trailing light.
He reaches for her
but she is gone
the door left open behind her.

How can there be so much light?
The clock shows midnight.
The sky is dark.
Only one star shining.
His cup is filled with memories
of when they were young,
the years given back.
He hopes she will come again
before time returns.
Before he knows he is dreaming,
and somewhere she is waiting,
and he can't recall the way.

In a Perfect Dream

I fell asleep to the song of the moon.
A harmonic rose-colored note and a rare blue.

Followed by the lavender of a dragonfly wing
and a tone of green.

Not an abrasive green
but like the most tender twig.

Each note a complete symphony.
Each color a finished painting.

A masterpiece as beguiling as the smile
of the Mona Lisa

inspiring as the glint from deep in her eye.
That spark which seduces

without losing power.
Maybe it was she who sang

not the moon.
The same soft lips barely moving.

A hum, a lullaby.
My eyes opened between this world

and the uncharted lands of Venus
which floated close by.

Circling me like a mother
I had not known.

Asking if this was enough.

A Day Trip Home

He pulled carrots up out of the earth.
The sound of roots letting go—vibrant
in the still afternoon.
Soil lifting with roots,
some thick—some fine as hair.
A sort of placenta.
Loose dirt—falling back to the ground.
Sweetness of carrot scent full in the air.
Crackle of paper bag as it was filled.

Both of our roots are in this earth.

Years later I will sit in his room
at the VA,
as he lies on his bed,
eyes closed to the world,
and wish we had talked.

But listen,
my senses were overwhelmed
when I stood with him in the middle of my life
on that land in Oklahoma.
Land his father had bought from the Choctaws.
Hear the jackrabbit thudding across the garden?
Cows in the pasture heads bowed,
lips to earth, pulling grass?
Whippoorwill's unrelenting call from the woods?
Brush of a crow crossing from pecan tree to apple tree?
Water slipping over rocks in the creek?

Silence filled with sound.
Here I knew everything.
I had no questions.

On this land—I am six years old again.
Bare feet busting hot clods of dirt,
following him on the same rows,
listening to the world.

I wish he had been the dad who sat down on that dirt with me,
pushed back my hair
and asked, "How is it really going?"
He was not. He was the dad that worked hard never swore.

He filled my paper sack to overflow
with food he had grown.
Told me to be safe and waved
as I backed out of the graveled drive.

There is plenty of time.

I think about these things
as he lies on his bed in the VA
curled on his side
like a question mark.
Eyes closed to all
the empty places
inside us.

Father and Child in Silhouette

I have a picture of us
as we walk a path at sunset.
The sun halos my hair.
I look up into your young, handsome face.
You hold my hand, smile at me.
All is lit rosy peach
by lowering light.
The path seems to go on forever.
Almost to touch eternity.

I remember us this way.

Now we have walked so far
our path has wandered
off the edge and around
as I reach for a hand
that trembles,
search clouded eyes
that look away
when you can't remember
my name.

The Crepe Myrtle Tree

I have read that we stay with our bodies
for three days after death.

When we viewed my father in his casket.
I saw his eyelashes move.
I told my husband.
He said he had noticed that too.
Listen: I have seen some of how we leave.
Go up, touch, come back.

Then on to exit:
One went through a hallway of stars.
One dropped a white rose as she left,
exclaimed it felt like Christmas there.
One was lifted among a million bubbles.
One cringed inside a cleansing light,
before being admitted.

I see my father in my vision, lighted
even under earth.
Body in place, not needed.
Free to go about the stars
with all knowledge of our universe.
He visits in my dreams.
We stand by a flowering tree.
He lets me know he understands our grief.
Takes a blossom, hands it to me.

Regrets

My grandma tells of hearing a band of angels
fly over the house the night before my mother died.
The evening of her death as twilight came,
turned the light to blue, purple and gold,
she knew her daughter's spirit waited
behind the bedroom door.
She stood there trying to remember
the words the angels sang.
If she opened the door
her daughter would be there.
She couldn't do it.
Her regrets
like stones.

Petal Pink Lips

I'm told there was a disagreement about whether
I should go to my mother's funeral.
Daddy said no and Grandma said yes.
Aunt Joan had dark hair like Mom,
was tall and thin like her.
When she put on my mother's green dress
I toddled after her crying.
Grandma convinced Daddy
I needed to say goodbye to my mother.
Grandma held me as we passed by the casket.
She tried to explain as much as she could
to a fifteen-month-old child.
I remember petal pink lips.
I had not seen my mother in days and when I did
I cried out to her, reached for her,
fell onto her.
As Grandma fell on the floor
I touched my mother one last time.

***

Grandma says I didn't walk enough
to dirty the bottoms of my shoes for the first year
after Mom died.
She said it was a good thing
because she wouldn't have been able
to take care of me otherwise.
When I began to walk again
my knees would fold, as in prayer,
and drop me full force onto the floor.
The doctor said I had a touch of rheumatic fever
and a little hole in my heart.

Meat

I remember Grandpa
with his three toothed smile.
From a chair by the kitchen window
I watch him.
He walks from the woods across the open pasture
to the back steps that led to the kitchen.
Grandma meets him there.
I look up at him.
With an apologetic look
he hands her his small bounty
of two dead squirrels.

Eyes level with theirs
I see the still shine
of the squirrels' brown eyes.
I see the stick handle they are carried by
through their feet.
I watch blood as it drips
from their noses onto the floor.
It makes red stars that trail after Grandma's shoes
across the scarred green and white linoleum.

I remember Grandma's grunt
as she lay them on the kitchen counter,
her silence as she slipped brown fur
from the carcasses,
the naked small bodies,
the bright smell of death
that spilled into the room.

I don't remember the taste
after it was rolled in cornmeal and fried
only the silence at the kitchen table while we ate.
The image sticks in my mind
like a cocklebur.
Sometimes it plays behind my eyes.
A silent movie with skips and static.
I feel a stab of empathy
for all of us.
Raw yet beautiful like
the blue and pink flesh of the meat.

Chicken Dinner

The brown hen
pecks in the grass,
keeps one golden eye turned
toward the white rooster.
He struts beside her
half as tall as me.
Grandma appears from the kitchen.
Pot is boiling.
Two swift hands enclose the hen.
Chicken alarms with loud squawks.
It is the only voice she has.
Grandma grips its neck close to the head.
Three loops through the air undoes neck bones,
brings the chicken down.
Life and death rattle around me
like marbles in a pickle jar.
On the ground the hen flops across the yard
circles my feet, follows me
no matter where I run.
Rooster moves around us with frantic screeches.
It's his job to protect the flock,
but nothing he can do.
Chicken lies still after one feeble gasp and spew.
Rooster herds others away across the yard.
His girl has disappeared, held by her feet,
head moving in useless sway
with Grandma's quick walk
back through the kitchen door.
Three dips into boiling water.
Loosened feathers that pull out in clumps
with a hollow sound.
Feathers in a bucket, head on top.
A clouded golden eye looks up at me.

In This Garden

I have planted my garden
finished with plenty of cabbage and kale.
The morning sun's light greets the soil,
welcomes leaves to peek above ground.
The air is warm, green, fresh.
My garden will be full.
A sparrow comes to find morsels
in the furrowed earth.
It looks my way,
seems to show gratitude.

I remember feeling thankful
when once I walked here with my grandmother
among rows we would tend and harvest.

We scattered seeds of varied shapes and sizes
into shallow trenches,
covering them and pressing the dirt.
She told me about the power of faith,
like a mustard seed, to move mountains.
She and I, knees in the rich earth,
holding the tiny, yellow seeds
that later would be leaves
filled with sustaining nourishment.

I had nothing to pray for then
but the faith she planted deep
waited.

Tie Loosely

Tie loosely what you would keep.
Tie with words, cupped hand,
breath against cheek.

A threat, a grasp, a bruising look will not bind.
Only things gently applied,
barely there, diaphanous—like light

twining through air.

When I First Held My Daughter

The nurse holds the placenta in front of me
as though it is a prize.
Tendrils of veins catch florescent light
waving about.
It seems to be telling my inadequate self
it's now my turn to nourish and care.

My mouth and body agape,
aching, swooning, shaking.
An infant's cry in the background of bustle.
The placenta is plopped into plastic,
carted away.

My child is placed in my arms,
mouth searching,
against my sweaty skin.
She is all tender flesh and need
bones still liquidy.

Her hunger finds the salty pearl she seeks,
and everything she will ever require from me
is in a sea that comes crashing through.

Swimming Lessons

I dropped her off for swim lessons and went shopping.
Took longer than I should.

When I returned she was at the hospital, had hit her head.
She had almost drowned.

I brought her home, lay her on her bed,
caressed her face.

Her eyes fluttered half open, swam with colors of the sea
as she asked *Are you my real mommy?*

I hesitated before answering. The moment whispered
I was not worthy.

Her golden hair splayed damply over her pillow in patterns
like Van Gogh's, *Starry Night*.

Of course I am. I lowered my lips,
branded my claim with a kiss onto her cool, rosy cheek.

It seemed she could be a child of the sea,
the lost daughter of Neptune,

balanced as she was
between earth and water.

From the edge of her pink bedspread,
with my eyes closed, I repeated, *of course I am.*

I Watch My Daughter Smoke

On a chair outside my window,
she leans back into the shadows
of the eaves.
A jacket pulled half on as though she can't decide
or doesn't care.
Her long hair flows over her shoulders.
Slim, tapered fingers
tipped with short, pink-painted nails
bring a cigarette to her lips.
Each time she inhales, daggers bury
into her precious throat,
bringing a rasp to her silk-on-velvet voice.
There is an odd beauty in this daring of destiny
as her lips part artfully to take the poison,
the smudge of red
on white paper
the sepia stain on her pale fingers.
Smoke curls in the air
through the waves of her hair,
leaves its sultry, acrid scent.
These ribbons, so thin, so binding.
If only I could gather her in,
hold her safe from this hateful vice
that taunts and threatens.
She takes another from the pack,
draws deeply.
Smoke dances about her.
A curse from her own lips.

The Shape of My Skin

I have things I don't want to let go.
Boxes of scribbles on scraps of paper
and filled note books.
Clothes I like, some I don't,
but keep.
Dishes I don't use.
The mirror that held my mother's image,
my grandmother's, now mine.

A huge chifforobe follows me
into houses large and small.
Memories of pets and people,
experiences good and bad.
A bank account, my name.

This menagerie of life's rituals
clings to me and I to it.
I have gathered these around.
They hold me in,
surround me like a skin.

Someday all will be tossed.
When I have nothing to say,
no need to cling.
This cup, these shoes,
that seashell.

The bird calling doesn't know
it was mentioned
when we said its name.

Neither will I.

I Think of You and Forget to Breathe

I'm not coming to the mountains again.
I've had too much high altitude
breathlessness.
The view is uninspiring.

The quiet unnerves me.
I notice the movement of mice
in the thickets, insects under logs
needles shifting in the pines.

Smells of wild flora and fauna strain my senses
I feel too close to the clouds.
But mainly it is that you aren't here
to point out the colors of the sky,

the far-away call of the condor,
close trill of the warbler,
your voice as you say the Latin names
of mosses we walk by,

I miss the things I will not notice
as I listen for your breath,
search for the scent of your hair
loose in the breeze after we swam.

You brushed it dry in the sun
until the shine almost burst my heart.
The heart that is too small to take in
the height and depth of these mountains all alone.

I consider the strange holiness of your absence
that finds me here looking for you
and forgetting to breathe.
I wake held by the stars.

Yellowed Crochet

We floated on the lake,
watched the stars cross the sky.
With each wave the rocks at the shore glistened
with moonlight,
Or was it our light?
I gripped your hand to hold me there.
Time was like sand back then.
Each grain an hour, day, month, never ending,
falling through us.

Happiness was pliable.
We ran gathering it, filling our pockets.
My skin was smooth, my hair flowed
long and shining behind me.
Each day a new door to open.

We didn't know time was passing, emptying
like an hourglass we could not turn.
No way to slow its cascade
when grains would be so few
we could count them.
No way to upend it before the last
would drop away.

***

Together, we have discovered time.
We have seen it grow our children.
We look into the bright faces
of our grandchildren they have brought.
Our parents have shown us how illness can come.
The mirrors on our walls refuse to lie.

Today as I climb the ladder into the attic
to visit the dust of my ancestors,
I reach for your hand to lift me.
In this house where I grew up
I feel the heaviness of what waits there.
Unlike years ago when I spent hours in fascination:
moving books, old letters, finding treasures
among the dust.

Time continues without my fore-bearers.
I am left to find proof of their existence
in these trunks and boxes of fragile, clinging things:
dolls with melted faces, books my dad read to me
faded and gnawed by mice.
other's strange, once-cherished possessions.
These have slept here for decades.

Now everything must be moved.
No one will live here when we have gone.
Those who left before reach to gather me
to their bosom.

I lift a piece of yellowed lace
crocheted by my great-grandmother.
I hold it up in the dim light of a window,
appreciate the tiny loops and swirls.
Touch where she touched.

In this darkening place
I need your arms to encircle me
as we look at those same stars,
to remind me which ones
we claimed as ours.

We Stop by the Lake Where You Once Proposed

The lake is low.
It ebbs and flows with the rain
Today it shows stones
we stepped on years ago.

Under those trees
the grass-covered floor
where we lay.
Do we wish we had chosen different ways?

You don't recall
you picked flowers for me
on the hill,
placed them one by one in my hair.

I remember the car wouldn't start
when we left the radio on
while dancing barefoot in the grass.
You say that was a different time.

Memory tells lies,
images detach, mingle.
The future we have
reveals itself second by second
like that sliver of moon lifting
above the cloud.

What will we remember of this day:
that last bright leaf hanging tight on the tree?
How you took my hand and we danced in silence
in the light shimmering at the edge of the Earth?

Angels in Paris

In Paris the air is so fine
at times angels can lower softly
from clouds and walk with
humans on the streets.

They often sit on top of buildings
seeming to prefer museums
and cathedrals.
You mostly see them around sunset
with peachy, golden hues
reflecting on their wings.

If you wave at them
they seem somewhat startled
they are noticed there
at all.

Jane's Eyes

Her eyes were cracked
like dropped marbles.
Blue like the sky they were opened to.
Her blouse undone
the circles of her breasts
absent of color.
Her gray hair still neatly coiffed.
She lay on the spring grass.
Five EMTs around her
standing, kneeling,
one holding her hand
silent and still
as in a saintly painting.
The tree above them cast its sheltering shadow.
Leaves like soft tongues whispered.

The couple ran a red light
that Sunday morning
My friend who hit them
had been on the way to my house.

I found myself in the husband's hospital room
offering condolences.
He wanted to know if Jane had suffered.
I told him she had not.
His exhaled relief made ripples
in the glass of water I offered.
I commented on his wife's blue eyes.

No, he said, *Jane had the most beautiful
brown eyes.*

I made my way to my car thinking
about Jane's eyes.
I wondered if I had glimpsed the heavens there
as she lifted above the trees and clouds
through the sky to wherever it is we go.

I returned to where she had lain.
I broke open a rose
and spread red petals
like a prayer.

Layers

She lies on a white sheeted bed in ICU.
Frail, curled onto her side.
Thin gray hair, thin hospital gown.
Everything about her
seems in fine layers
all the way past the faint beat
of her heart.
Her back to the world,
her only armor.

He stands, young man, feet planted
on sterile tiles.
Watches her
through the large glass window.
He seems deep in his thoughts
waiting.

I find myself waiting too.
So still, barely breathing,
knowing

if she uncurls even a little
the layers will come apart,
drift up one after the other
to wherever it is an old woman goes
when she has lost too much
of herself
to remain tethered.

Falling

The man falling
from a tall building
knows when his life will end.

There are things we don't want
to touch.
We tell these in a quiet way.

Say, thinking of a child's face
surrounding this moment.
Clouds drift, ocean waves
shh, shh.

We are all falling.
Something will stop our fall.
The body will shatter into fragments
like starlight.

Lifting. Lifting.

The Pain Body

The Pain Body is a cumulative entity of all our previous psychological and emotional trauma from our infancy to our present.
—Eckhart Tolle

When I was a child I fantasized
digging a place in the soft floor
of the woods behind our house
covering myself with sticks and branches
hiding there to wait until they called my name:
I wouldn't answer
but lie straight and still
while darkness came
shutting out the world.
My pain would shift
to those calling me.
Their hollow voices circling the trees.

After my mother's death
there was a new wife
and I was a leftover piece.
My mothers' name brought sorrow
It was said rarely and in whispers.
I felt uncomfortable when I heard it
as if I had done something wrong
like I was a cause of their pain.
A child-shaped wound that
wouldn't heal.

I never dug that hole.
What if no one came to find me?
No one called my name?
My hurt would multiply.
I thought of a rat I had seen
in the field after harvest.
It lay lifeless, blood on its head,
its eyes closed.
Ants were finding it.
I touched its bare, gray tail
to pull it away.
It opened one eye
observed me briefly
closed it with almost a wink.
Seeming so wise.
Holding its pain.

Searching

I arrived in my mother's arms as if untouched.
Soon I needed the caress of her skin:
its warmth, its scent of roses, milk
and tinge of secret tobacco.
Her voice resonated through me
imprinting on me, waking me into life.
Then she was gone.

I was left to discover the world alone.
Knowing her in fragments of dreams
and stories overheard.
She was like a summer breeze
that brushed by and went still.

Later she became my torment.
I was afraid of meeting her in the dark hallway.
Afraid of what she might look like now.
She was the ghost under my bed, waiting.
The distant voice reaching in the night.

After more than two decades I brought out her picture.
Within the portrait of soft blacks and shades of white
I searched for who she had been.
But what did I really want?
The missing parts of myself I would never know.
She held them bound inside her still heart
beneath folded hands.

My fingers moved gently across her features
I see she was only a girl.
It seems she was looking back at me
thinking how I have grown.
Her skin, her eyes and smile younger than mine.
Tell me your story, I whisper.

When I take a drowning beetle from the water,
wrest a bird from a cat's claws, it is her I rescue.
If I say a silent prayer for an animal on the road
gone hard and flat in the sun it's her I'm mourning.
When in the quiet I take my pen, extract found bits of her,
print them in words on paper, I am willing her to breathe,
step into the room and save me.

Barefoot with Angels

An image of my
      fingerprint

floats against
      a dark void.

Bright swirls
      blue, purple, violet

vibrating
      inviting.

I touch the colors
      A voice surrounds me.

See how easily you can reach
      past the veil?

It's just like pushing
      through air.

***

I feel her touch.
My mother stands close.
My bare toes grip the edge of reality.
I feel I am fully trespassing.

Winged forms glimmer inside a room
filled with a rosy mist.
I hear conversation in a language like song.
Tempered laughter and a feeling of mirth
circles through.

As though she is mentioning the weather,
she motions, *Come on, let's go walk with the angels.*
It's tempting.
She reaches her hand to me.
My toes begin to release their hold.
Hurry, you know you can't stay long.
This is only a dream.
Her words draw open the curtains of sleep.
The visit dissolves into sunlit dust.
My feet are light as glitter all day.

The Color of Her Eyes

She waits for me to close my eyes.
arrives in a car, invites me in.
Her words flow, dream-like
from the drivers seat
to me in the back.
My mother, the teen she had been,
tells me her favorite color was pink;

I had some lipstick the color of strawberries.
I liked to wear it especially with my baby pink dress.
Your dad thought lipstick looked "trampy,"
but I knew he liked it in a way.
To please him I wiped it so it was lighter
but I still wore it.
I would put it on real dark
admire it in the mirror before I blotted it pink.

I also liked the color green.
I looked good in it
and had a minty-green dress I wore a lot.
My eyes were green with brown in them.
Once, I was driving and looked in the car mirror.
the sun hit my face.
I saw gold flecks shining in my eyes.
It flashed through my mind,
I didn't know who I really was,
or who those eyes belonged to.
I didn't know that my last breath
was so close.

Her voice goes silent.
I'm left outside the car.
I hear only the crackle of stones
catching and releasing as she drives over them.
It's a sound like an old forty-five record
at the ending of a song.

I had always wondered
about the color of her eyes.

These Bones I Carry

Each time I visited my grandma I asked to look through her picture
　　box
I studied the photos of my mother.
Sifted contrasts of darkness and light.
Followed the lines of her body.
I wanted to look through the ocean of time to see her, to know her.
Nothing gave a hint of what a brief life she would have.
So brief I had no memories of her.
Any image, touch, or sound, irretrievable.
I found only an absence that leaves me at the edge of a dark void.
The child lost in a forest.
All she would have told me unsaid.
In photographs of her I see a young wife, a teenager unsure.
A lilt of her lip as she smiles.
The shape of her eyes, line of her jaw.
A deep wave at her forehead of dark, fine hair.
I note thin legs gracefully posed.
The curve of her hips.
Her delicate hands.

As I search the treasures in Grandma's box of pictures
there is one that always stops me.
A small black and white photo.
I pick it up by an edge,
admire my mother's neatly pressed flower print dress,
the proud smile as she holds my twin cousins
tucked in the crooks of her arms.
I was envious of those two she nestles close.
There is no picture from the year we had together
of her holding me.
The desire for some sign of her nurture seeps through my years.

One day as I stare at that picture
Grandma tells me my mother was pregnant with me
when it was taken.
I look more closely at the picture
notice the small roundness of her belly below her belted waist.
I imagine a fetal me curled like a kitten inside.
Her smile could be for the child growing there.
Grandma takes another picture from the box.
A toddler on a chair squinting into the sun.
I see my mother's delicate fingers on my shoulder
holding me safe.

My Mother in Half Shadow

After years of absence
she visits
in a half-shadowed dream
like the memory of a memory.
She drops a dusty quilt
from around her.
Wraps herself in the soft white curtains
that blow at my window.

As familiar as my own, her voice floats
through the moonlight between us:

I have not left you
My hand is in the wind
that brushes against your skin
I lead you to where sweet earth
lies under your feet .
I speak with you through the language
of stars as you sleep

She smiles.
Do you know me?
I know her smile,
It holds our secrets.
"Yes"
My whisper follows her
as she unwraps from the curtain
slips back into air.

Like a Sip of Wine

As this day of blues,
golden leaves, autumn air swirls around us
moves through
I gather it.

As time passes I will remember
the movement of your hand
as you point to silver spiderwebs drifting.
Your voice resonant
as you note the falling leaves.

I smell the moist earth,
feel the smooth touch of your skin.

Half a moon, half a year,
half a life recedes.
Shadows of clouds
reflections on water
a whippoorwill's call
slide away.

This time stays.

Your image comes to me
like a sip of wine
across time
opens my laughter
wakes me from slumber.

Closes the space
between us.

About the Author

Linda Hughes has a BA in advertising and journalism. Her years working as a licensed massage therapist helped her develop her natural tendencies of empathy and intuition, which often are revealed in her writing.

Her poetry has been published in many literary magazines, including: *The Orchards Poetry Journal, Plainsongs Literary Magazine, Humana Obscura, Evening Street Review, Halcyon Days, California Quarterly, Avalon Literary Review, Main Street Rag, Poetry South, American Journal of Nursing's Art of Nursing, Door Is a Jar,* and others.

She has worked at a Pulitzer Prize-winning news publication in Florida. Her roots are in Oklahoma. Now she makes her home in Florida where she enjoys being surprised by animals that wander out from the jungle and pass through her yard.

www.ingramcontent.com/pod-product-compliance
Lightning Source LLC
Chambersburg PA
CBHW071013160426
43193CB00012B/2038